PETER PAUL RUBENS

RUBENS

Philippe de Montebello

Department of European Paintings

Metropolitan Museum of Art

McGRAW-HILL BOOK COMPANY · NEW YORK · LONDON · TORONTO · SYDNEY

Cover picture, *Woman with Crossed Hands*, detail (c. 1630), red, black, and white chalk drawing, Boymans-van Beuningen Museum, Rotterdam. Photographs for Figures 2 and 4, courtesy Alinari. Photographs for Figure 3, courtesy MAS Reproducciones. Photograph for Figure 13, courtesy Giraudon.

PETER PAUL RUBENS, painter, diplomat, man of learning, was one of those rare figures in the history of art who completely dominated their age. He combined an indefatigable, enterprising spirit with enormous creative energy which he channeled in many directions, becoming deeply involved in the intellectual, political, and spiritual life of his country. As a diplomat, he was continuously engaged in negotiations to bring peace to war-torn Flanders. As an artist, his dynamic, exuberant, and sensual Baroque style swept aside the prevailing currents, and all painters reshaped their way of seeing in his image. Even such independent and strong artistic personalities as Jacob Jordaens and Anthony Van Dyck were profoundly affected by his art.

When in 1609 Rubens returned from eight years of study in Italy to astound Flanders with his large canvases that were, in his own words, "the glorification of the forces and aspirations of man," the artistic climate there was distinctly temperate. There were many fine painters, but none with a dominating artistic personality or gifted with true genius. The "Romanists," so called because they derived their art from Roman Mannerism, constituted the main current; their dean had been Frans Floris (c. 1516-1570), and he was followed by such painters as Michel Coxcie, Marten de Vos, Otto Vaenius, Hendrick de Clerck, and Abraham Janssens, who was perhaps the most gifted of all. But nothing in their mannered, stilted art presaged the sublime canvases of Rubens, so pulsating with life. Only Joachim Beuckelaer (1533-1573) anticipated him; his kitchen genre scenes are dominated by a warm red and gold palette, and the solidly painted figures have some of Rubens' healthy vitality.

Alongside these Italianate painters worked a host of other artists, more typically Flemish in their avoidance of the monumental in favor of the minute; they studied the visible world at close range and meticulously reproduced it in small pictures of considerable charm and fantasy. Many were specialists: Ambrosius Bosschaert, for example, painted flowers; Van Coninxloo did landscapes; and Jan "Velvet" Brueghel, the most able and versatile, could paint all the wonders of the universe—shells, flowers, trees, the birds of paradise, and the

Frontispiece.
Self-Portrait (1635-1640)
black and white chalk
on light-brown paper
8" x 6¼"
Royal Library, Windsor Castle

[Facing this page]
Detail of
Studies for a Kermesse
British Museum, London

fish of the sea. But all these artists painted only fragments of life. It was Rubens who captured it in its totality, who harnessed its most dynamic forces to present us with an image of the world in constant flux and renewal, where God is the prime mover and man is shown in all the exaltation of his physical being.

Rubens' magnificent Baroque style and deep religious convictions made him the greatest exponent of the Counter-Reformation in the north, and he set out to inspire the faithful with strikingly realistic images of great dramatic power—martyrdoms and scenes of the Passion, or glorious and exalted portrayals honoring the new saints of the militant church, Ignatius of Loyola, Charles Borromeo, or Francis of Assisi. His own personal piety became the supreme expression of Christianity in Flanders, lush and popular in contrast to the mysticism of El Greco, the tenderness and gravity of Poussin, or the introspection of Rembrandt. Rubens used sumptuousness in reaction to the austerity of Protestantism, and his deliberately ostentatious, lyrical, and opulent altarpieces proclaim noisily, forcibly, and with unconcealed proselytism, the glory of God.

Rubens molded life with the clay of optimism; he reproduced its fundamental rhythms in pictures of sheer pictorial brilliance in which the whole process of his inventive genius, exuberance, and love of life are transmitted in the brushwork; its daring, variety, and verve equal that of his subjects to complete a synthetic unity that is the triumph of Baroque painting. Rubens' sense of purpose in life comes through very strongly in these works, which are clearly those of one of the most outgoing and positive artists in history. This is why, although he lived in most turbulent times, there is never disquiet or anguish in his art, never a tormented image, never a hint of decay.

Rubens, however, was deeply concerned with the plight of his beloved Flanders which, throughout his life, was ravaged by a bloody war. The original Netherlandish revolt against Spanish rule had been transformed into a political and religious conflict between the northern or United Provinces (Holland) and the southern provinces (Flanders). Able to withstand reconquest by Catholic Spain because of superior sea power, the United Provinces became increasingly independent and Protestant, while Flanders was quickly subdued and thereafter remained loyal to Catholicism and to Spain. Though they signed a treaty of union in 1577, it lasted a scant two years; each side then proclaimed its autonomy, the north led by William of Orange, with the backing of France and England, and the south under the continued administration of Spain. Each claiming the other's territory, they fought a long and bitter war which eventually became part of a total European conflict, the Thirty Years War. Peace was achieved only in 1648 when both sides accepted a stalemate and Spain recognized Dutch independence. The Flemings had sought a lasting peace from 1598 to 1633 while under the sovereignty of Archduke Albert of Austria, and later of his widow the Infanta Isabella, to whom her father, Philip II of Spain, had given the Netherlands as a dowry; but the truce of 1609 lasted only twelve years. Once again the port of Antwerp was ruined by a Dutch blockade of the river Scheldt, and the Flemish countryside, the battleground for the major European powers, was ravaged by foreign armies.

Although he was above all else a painter, Rubens was to devote most of his energies, both through his art and political activity, towards seeking a permanent peace. Since he enjoyed the full confidence of Isabella and had a clear grasp of the political situation in Europe, he was sent on numerous diplomatic missions to secure support for the Flemish position. His fame as a painter offered him entry to the principal courts of Europe, all eager to engage his services, and his aristocratic bearing and knowledge of letters and science assured him of a good reception.

Even Rubens' birth was somehow tied to the political scene. His father, Jan Rubens, a prominent lawyer and alderman of Antwerp, was a Calvinist. At the height of Philip II's persecutions of Protestants, he and his wife, Marie Pypelinckx, were forced to escape to Germany. Sometime before 1570, they settled in Cologne. There Jan Rubens was befriended by Anna of Saxony, the second wife of William of Orange, who earlier had also fled to Germany as he opposed Philip's persecutions in Orange and Holland. Unfortunately, Jan Rubens and Anna were charged with adultery by Anna's brother-in-law, Count John of Nassau. Since adultery was a crime punishable by death, it is probable that Jan Rubens would have been executed had his liaison been with any other. However, the ruling family of the United Provinces could not afford a scandal, and Jan Rubens was simply and quietly jailed. Marie's correspondence with her imprisoned husband shows great polish, courage, and magnanimity, and Rubens' own strength of character and probity, so vaunted by his contemporaries, may well be owed to her. Mainly thanks to the impassioned entreaties of his wife, Jan was soon pardoned and exiled to Siegen in Westphalia. It was there, in 1577, that Peter Paul Rubens was born.

After Jan Rubens died in exile in Germany, Marie and her children, all devout Catholics, returned to Antwerp in 1589. At first Peter Paul attended a Latin school where he studied the classics; later, when financial difficulties forced him to withdraw from school, he was taken in as a page in the household of Countess Marguerite de Ligne d'Arenberg, where he became acquainted with court etiquette and the ways of the nobility; both were to prove invaluable to him during the course of his diplomatic career.

Rubens was to study painting with three masters. At the age of fourteen, he studied with his uncle-by-marriage, the *retardataire* landscapist Tobias Verhaeght; then for three years with Adam van Noort, who was also the master of Jacob Jordaens; and next with Otto Vaenius, pupil of the Italian Mannerist Federico Zuccaro and court painter to Archduke Albert. Though there was probably little of spiritual inspiration that Rubens could have derived from his apprenticeship with these masters, during those eight years of study he thoroughly learned the craft of painting. In 1598 he became a free master in the guild of St. Luke, remained in Antwerp two more years, and in 1600 left for Italy.

Very little is known of Rubens' activities during these two years in Antwerp, but this is not especially serious since it is really what he produces after his return from Italy in 1609 that will revolutionize painting in Flanders and have such a huge impact outside its borders. For a clue to what the young Rubens produced, however, we must look at the art of his

Figure 1.
Hendrick de Clerck
(c. 1570-1629)
The Descent from the Cross
(1628)
Musées Royaux des Beaux-Arts
Brussels

teachers and their contemporaries, such as Hendrick de Clerck (Figure 1), for Rubens' works of this period are probably not too different from theirs. In a painting recently attributed to Rubens, the *Cain and Abel* in the Blois Museum, the rigid drawing, restricted picture space, and disruptive lighting give little hint of the marvels to come. In many ways this Mannerist composition is the antithesis of Rubens' later Baroque style in which every element—deep, diagonally recessive space; free, loose brushwork and drawing; unifying light; and strong, sweeping rhythms—creates an intensely expressive and emotional statement in which the beholder is made to participate fully.

It is during Rubens' eight years in Italy, while under the influence of Michelangelo and the Venetian colorists, that his style will begin to round out and bloom into fully developed Baroque. Although Rubens had seen Italian works in Flanders and knew many others through engravings, most important for his career were the vast decorations which he was able to study at first hand; his manner of painting was to become much broader and grander than anything previously done in Flanders, where painting on a large scale was literally unknown.

Rubens probably went to Italy for several reasons. First, the trip was then considered an essential part of a painter's training; but equally important, he saw no real chance for advancement in Antwerp, which around 1600 had not recovered from the last war and had a somber future. Still, it is fairly certain that Rubens must have had a considerable reputation even before his departure for Italy, for soon after his arrival there he was chosen to be court painter by the twenty-seven-year-old Vincenzo Gonzaga, Duke of Mantua, whose court was one of the most enlightened in Europe. Vincenzo, for example, corresponded regularly with Galileo, and his court musician was the great Monteverdi.

Rubens must have been most flattered and delighted with this appointment; it gave him a chance to study the duke's famous collections and the decorations of the Roman Mannerist Giulio Romano in the Palazzo del Tè, as well as to meet with the high aristocracy and men of letters and science. Once Rubens put aside his brush for the day, he preferred the company of scholars and humanists and avoided fellow artists, especially those from the north whom he considered too bohemian. Later he was to record this preference in a remarkable portrait which showed him listening, along with his brother Philip and Juan den Wouwère, to the humanist teacher Justus Lipsius (Figure 2).

Rubens quickly won the duke's confidence and was sent as a special envoy to Madrid in 1603 to deliver some paintings to the Spanish court; although a very minor one, this was the first of his numerous diplomatic missions. In Madrid he painted a series of life-sized apostles, which are strongly modeled and vigorous, and, more important, a most original and striking equestrian portrait of the Duke of Lerma (Figure 3); instead of the customary profile view, rider and horse are shown almost full front, creating a dramatic diagonal into space.

The most important commission Rubens received in Italy was for the main altarpiece of the Jesuit church in Mantua, *The Holy Trinity Adored by the Gonzaga Family,* which

9

Figure 2.
The Four Philosophers
(1612-1614)
oil on wood
64½″ x 54¾″
Palazzo Pitti
Florence

Figure 3.
The Duke of Lerma
(1603)
oil on canvas
114" x 81"
Medinaceli Convent
Madrid

Figure 4.
Francesco IV of Gonzaga
fragment from *The Holy Trinity*
Adored by the Gonzaga Family
(1604-1605), oil on canvas
26⅓″ x 20¼″
Kunsthistorisches Museum
Vienna

already shows the influence of Titian, especially in the color. Unfortunately, the altarpiece was cut into pieces at the time of the French Revolution, but in the fragments which remain (Figure 4) the portraits of the donors are far more powerful, modern, and alive than the stiff effigies painted by his Flemish contemporary at the Duke's court, Frans Pourbus the Younger (Figure 5). *The Baptism of Christ* (Figure 6), also painted for the Jesuit church, shows how he assimilated the art of other Italian Renaissance masters; the powerful forms reveal direct borrowings from Michelangelo and Raphael, and the deep, rich color and restless light indicate the influence of Tintoretto.

We know that Rubens made numerous copies after Italian masters and antique statuary, and that he occasionally referred to them for his own compositions; but, apart from pure scholarly interest, there are few painters for whom it is more irrelevant to hunt for specific borrowings. Everything that Rubens took from others he assimilated totally into his immensely original and personal style, and no shred of the spirit of his sources ever remains; all he touches becomes pure Rubens. He even frequently reworked and "corrected" other masters' drawings and prints in his private collection, always with an end to increasing the movement and accentuating the expression.

In 1608 Rubens departed in a rush for Antwerp upon hearing news of his mother's failing health; unfortunately, he arrived too late. Despite the urgings of the Duke of Mantua and his own desire to return, Rubens was never again to visit Italy, though he later traveled extensively in many other countries, combining painting with diplomatic work.

Rubens' fame had preceded his return to Antwerp. Almost immediately he was appointed court painter to the Hapsburg archduke and archduchess. However, he received special dispensation to reside in Antwerp rather than at the court in Brussels. As he confessed to a friend, he had "little inclination to become once more a courtier." Though he painted a great deal for his patrons, notably their portraits, he also received many commissions from private citizens and from the town of Antwerp. Times were once again ripe for lucrative commissions; the twelve-year truce with the United Provinces, begun in 1609, restored some semblance of quiet and prosperity to the torn country, and the countless pictures which had been destroyed during the iconoclastic excesses of the religious wars now had to be replaced.

In October 1609, Rubens made the first of his two happy marriages, taking as his bride, Isabella Brant, the daughter of a prominent Antwerp lawyer and humanist, and with whom he was to have three children. Very soon after the wedding he painted a beautiful though strangely mannered ceremonial portrait of himself and Isabella, rather exotic in color, yet unusually reserved and self-conscious in feeling (Figure 7).

At first the young couple shared a house with Rubens' brilliant brother Philip, who was active in public affairs in Antwerp and helped Rubens in making valuable contacts. But Philip died suddenly in 1610, and Rubens then set up his studio in his father-in-law's house. The deluge of commissions coming his way, however, necessitated larger quarters and Rubens soon built a studio outside the city. Little by little, after he made the studio his home, Rubens

Figure 6.
The Baptism of Christ (1604-1606)
oil on canvas, 161¾" x 265¾"
Musée Royal des Beaux-Arts, Antwerp

Figure 5.
Frans Pourbus the Younger (c. 1570-1622)
Portrait of Pierre Ricardus (1592)
oil on wood, 42⅛" x 30⅓"
Groeningemuseum, Bruges

Figure 7.
Rubens and Isabella Brant
(1609-1610)
oil on canvas, 70½″ x 53½″
Alte Pinakothek, Munich

transformed it into a veritable palace to house his vast collections of pictures and precious objects, including the valuable antique marbles he was to purchase from Sir Dudley Carleton in 1618. His house was long one of the principal sights of Antwerp and has recently been restored.

Fortunately, we know a little about Rubens' daily routine during these years from an account by the engraver Roger de Piles:

> Though there seemed to be much distraction in his way of life, yet his habits were for all that very regular. He rose every morning at four and made it a rule to begin his day by hearing Mass, except when he was hindered by the gout that incommoded him much. After that he fell to work, having always by him a reader who was in his pay and who read some good books: Plutarch very often, or Livy or Seneca. As he was devoted to his profession, he ordered his diet so as to be able to work with ease, and this is why he ate very little at dinner for fear lest the vapors of the meat should hinder the application to the work at hand or his application again hinder the digestion of the meat. He painted thus up to five in the evening, when he mounted his horse to take the air outside the town or upon the ramparts. At other times he would seek other relaxation for his mind. On his return from his promenade he would as a rule find in his house one or more of his friends who had come in to sup with him and who contributed to the pleasure of the table. He, nevertheless, held in great aversion any excess in drink or good cheer. His greatest pleasure was to mount some fair Spanish horse, to read in some book, or to pass in review the medals, the agates, carnelians, and other engraved gems of which he had a fine collection.

It is significant that Rubens is said to have hated excess, for at first glance his works might suggest the contrary. They are impassioned and exuberant, overpowering and frenzied in content. Yet we feel strongly that they are governed by a clear intellect, and, as we see, Rubens led an ordered life guided by high moral standards. Indeed, the verses from Juvenal, which he had carved upon the pavilion standing in his garden, would have pleased his friend Justus Lipsius, a great teacher of Stoicism: "Let your prayer be for a healthy mind in a healthy body; pray for a brave heart that knows not the fear of death and is innocent of guile and cupidity"; "Leave it to the Gods themselves to provide what is good for us and what will be serviceable for our state; for in place of what is pleasing they will give us what is best. Man is dearer to them than he is to himself." These verses were most appropriate as the motto for one of the leading exponents in the north of the Christian humanism popular during the Counter-Reformation; all his life, Rubens was to be faithful to its precept calling for the domination of the passions and its philosophy of moral duty based on the teachings of both the Stoic philosopher Seneca and the Catholic Church.

During his first decade in Antwerp, Rubens, always an indefatigable worker, produced a tremendous quantity of allegorical, historical, biblical, and mythological subjects; they offered a great variety of different themes, variations, and challenges for his inexhaustible and ever active imagination. Biblical and pagan subjects alike afforded him opportunities to brush into most of his canvases luxurious nudes and powerfully built men, a chance to contrast sinew with the opulent, enticing flesh of his women, of which his two wives are the archetypes: plump and sensual, they exude, so to speak, their powers of regeneration by their health and vitality, and their glowing skin has been rendered by Rubens with the most succulent lacteous and carnate tones. One of the early pictures where these qualities are shown to best effect is the marvelous *Toilet of Venus* with its inimitable nacreous tones (Figure 8). The *St. Sebastian* in Berlin or the *Juno and Argus* in Cologne are vigorous paintings in which the male body is boldly foreshortened, full of intensity and brute strength. These pictures are strongly modeled and solidly painted, with heavy draperies and massive, well-defined forms; the deeply saturated colors, often quite raw, are applied in broad, flat areas, the whole giving an impression of great power and at the same time of great solidity. There is an assurance in the composition, in the daringly accented highlights and shadows, and in the firmly defined contours that already singles out Rubens as a giant among a host of timid craftsmen.

From the start Rubens worked on a heroic scale, painting huge altarpieces in which he could pour out his inventive genius. Without false modesty he wrote to William Trumbull, an agent of Charles I: "I am by inclination better suited to paint on a large scale than small pictures. Each has his specialty; my talent is such that no undertaking, no matter how large or complex, has taxed my courage."

What is most significant during the years of Rubens' production until about 1618 is the variety of his painting styles. We note almost a hesitation in his works as he alternates and wavers between the loose pictorial manner he will later adopt wholeheartedly and a more careful and measured Baroque style. It is startling to see pictures done in a bold, free manner followed almost immediately by more traditional ones which strive for the high finish and polish of the Italianizers. But we must not lose sight of the overwhelming effect his daring works must have produced on people attuned to the mannered painting of a Hendrick de Clerck. Indeed, the simple explanation is that Rubens, hungry for fame and fortune, must have deliberately exercised caution in certain commissions in order to avoid antagonizing his patrons. It must have been as much of a shock for the citizens of Antwerp to see the swirling, brilliantly colored, bold new forms of Rubens' altarpieces, overflowing with life, as it was for the Parisians of the 1870s, used to the slick productions of the Salon painters, to see the revolutionary works of the Impressionists.

Among the first altarpieces is the enormous *Raising of the Cross* (Figure 9) commissioned in 1610 for the Cathedral of Antwerp. The exploding diagonal composition, the bold sweep of movement and recession make this one of the first completely Baroque pictures. Such a work, so pulsating with life and dynamism, must have shocked Rubens' contemporaries. But, as we said, Rubens compromised with existing sponsorship, and *The Raising of the Cross* turns out to be more advanced in many ways than a triptych painted three or four years later, *The Doubting of Thomas* (Figure 10), the wings of which bear fine donor

Figure 8.
The Toilet of Venus
(c. 1613-1615)
oil on wood
48¾″ x 38½″
Liechtenstein Gallery
Vaduz

Figure 10.
The Doubting of Thomas (1613-1615)
oil on wood, 56¼″ x 48½″
Musée Royal des Beaux-Arts, Antwerp

Figure 9.
The Raising of the Cross (1610-1611)
oil on wood, 182″ x 134¼″
Antwerp Cathedral

21

portraits of Rubens' friends the burgomaster of Antwerp Nicolas Rockox and his wife. Painted in the strong, plastic, Italianate manner, it is an example of Rubens' so-called "classic" style; flesh is firm and gleaming, the surface highly finished, the composition parallel to the picture plane. *The Descent from the Cross* (Slide 1) is likewise more tradition-oriented; though boldly original in composition, it has been given a polished surface, again probably to appease the conservative tastes of Rubens' patrons. Yet one only need compare it to the trite, totally conventional *Descent from the Cross* by Hendrick de Clerck (Figure 1) to appreciate all that is nevertheless new, true, and dynamic in the inspired work of Rubens.

Rubens' activity during these years leaves one breathless. It is almost beyond belief that any one man could have been responsible for so much, even though he did have help from the many assistants in his studio. We must continually keep in mind that Rubens produced a great many more canvases and masterminded many more projects than those touched upon in this book; to speak of any one field at too great length or without some interruption is to limit Rubens' prodigious activity. Besides painting, he made cartoons for tapestries, furnished designs for sculptors and architects, drew extensively for printmakers, and produced designs for books, illustrations, and frontispieces. Interestingly enough, Rubens' designs for books and engravings are rather restrained and classical in spirit, and we are not in the least surprised to learn that he never etched a plate or scratched the copper himself; the medium was simply too limiting and constricting to suit his expansive temperament.

In these years Rubens gave himself wholeheartedly to the exuberant full Baroque style already strongly revealed by *The Raising of the Cross* and painted a number of his most dynamic and spirited works, including such titanesque subjects as the Last Judgment, the Fall of the Damned, and the Battle of the Amazons. In *The Fall of the Damned* (Figure 11) he rivals Michelangelo's *Last Judgment* in the Sistine Chapel, but in the difference between these works lies the key to Rubens' genius: whereas the Italian artist treated each figure as an entity radiating its own power, Rubens has concentrated on the whole; the power no longer comes from each figure, but from the fusion of all the bodies, from the overall whirlwind of movement. While Michelangelo boldly set one colossal figure after another in an ensemble of overpowering though essentially static strength, here the damned are not perched on clouds or individually delineated, but cascade down in clusters, spiralling in a frenzied avalanche of writhing bodies, a pictorial eddy of unparalleled fury and brilliance.

However, it was not only through paintings like the heroic and realistic *Descent from the Cross* or *The Fall of the Damned,* so full of movement, that Rubens served the ends of the Counter-Reformation. Capable of great nuances of feeling and execution, he also expressed a more intimate and tender form of piety in his small Madonnas smiling gently at the world and surrounded by cherubs and flower garlands (Slide 4). It is a truly inward, complex, and deeply felt religious feeling that emanates from the beautiful *Last Communion of Saint Francis,* one of Rubens' most coherent and completely synthesized pictures (Figure 12).

Figure 11.
The Fall of the Damned
(1618-1620)
oil on wood, 72″ x 46¾″
Alte Pinakothek, Munich

Figure 12.
The Last Communion of Saint Francis
(1619)
oil on wood, 166″ x 89″
Musée Royal des Beaux-Arts, Antwerp

The almost limp body of the saint has a truth and directness that is really moving, even poignant, and strangely devoid of the usual rhetoric found in seventeenth-century religious painting.

The Last Communion of Saint Francis well illustrates Rubens' ability to build great harmonies of color with a restricted palette instead of his usual strong and bright tones, for the picture is full of subtle color nuances, a glorious harmony of muted reds, greens, and brown golds. Actually, a general warming up of Rubens' colors has been noted around this time, and some have attributed it to the influence of the master's most gifted assistant, Anthony Van Dyck, who worked in his studio from 1617 to 1621. The hardness of the early works is gone, replaced by a more fluid and pictorial conception; the paint is more thinly applied with looser, more daring and rapid brushwork well suited to the swift execution necessary for many vast and demanding commissions. We know from an eyewitness, in fact, that Rubens began to thin his paint with increasing amounts of turpentine. Among the most glorious of the works done in this new, totally liberated style is *Le Coup de Lance* (Slide 5); its heroic and robust grandeur make it one of the greatest—and certainly the grandest—Crucifixions ever painted.

During the early twenties Rubens seems to have neglected pagan themes in favor of a staggering number of religious works. A true champion of the Catholic Church, Rubens was asked in 1620 to produce thirty-nine separate pictures for the Jesuit church Saint Charles Borromeo in Antwerp. In the contract it was clearly stated that the sketches, that is, the compositions, were to be his, although the finished works could be executed by students. Many of these small preliminary sketches survive, and they are entirely from Rubens' hand (Figure 13). Like all his sketches they are most precious in that they reveal intimately and forcefully the creative process of the painter. They are the overriding evidence of Rubens' unbelievable rapidity and power of suggestion; with the sparsest of means—a few lines and splashes of color dashed onto the panel—he is able to convey fully all the action, all the movement of a particular subject. The sketches demanded great skill in foreshortening and bear further witness to the artist's incredible virtuosity. Many of them, such as *The Raising of the Cross,* are full of such violent movement and are treated with such irresistible force and conviction that, although the church was destroyed by fire in 1718, one can still imagine the paintings sweeping the faithful into real religious fervor, precisely as they were designed to do.

In many cases, such as the cycle for Saint Charles Borromeo, we know from the contracts that students executed all or part of the finished compositions. This participation is corroborated by Rubens' own testimony and by reports of eyewitnesses such as Otto Sperling, a Danish physician who visited Rubens' studio in 1621. Sperling wrote that he saw in one room "many young painters who worked on different pictures on which Rubens had drawn with chalk and put a spot of color here and there; the young men had to execute the paintings which were then finished off with lines and colors by Rubens himself." In a letter of 1618 to the English collector-diplomat Sir Dudley Carleton, Rubens also gives us a clear picture

Figure 13.
The Raising of the Cross (1620)
oil on wood, 13″ x 15″
Louvre, Paris

of the role played by assistants. Listing the pictures which he is offering Sir Dudley in exchange for antiquities, he describes one as "original, the whole by my hand"; another as "original, by my hand, except a most beautiful landscape done by the hand of a master skillful in the genre"; and yet another as "commenced by one of my pupils . . . but all retouched by my hand."

Nevertheless, the extent of workshop participation in Rubens' *oeuvre* is not precisely known. On the basis of style and quality we can often distinguish the hand of the master from that of a pupil; but there is no clear-cut rule and curiously enough, while some relatively small paintings obviously lack the Rubens touch, some of the largest altarpieces appear to be entirely his own work. To add to the confusion, many of Rubens' assistants were proficient painters who often executed paintings outside of the workshop, which still abound in Belgian churches.

While most of the assistants who did the tedious groundwork in Rubens' pictures are anonymous, Rubens also enlisted the help of very fine independent artists to complete certain parts in his paintings which were their specialty. Among these collaborators were Frans Snyders who painted animals, Lucas van Uden who brushed in landscape backgrounds, and Jan "Velvet" Brueghel who painted the flower garland in the *Madonna and Child* (Slide 4) and the flora and fauna in the *Feast of Achelous* in the Metropolitan Museum, New York.

The year 1621 was an important year in Rubens' career, for once again the course of his life was to be altered by changes in the political scene. Within three months both Philip III and Archduke Albert died, and the twelve-year truce between the United Provinces and Spanish Flanders ended. Flanders once more was torn and ravaged by war. As a man of the world with contacts in many high places and in sympathy with Isabella's fervent wish to end the war, Rubens was ideally suited for the post of ambassador-at-large. For the next few years he was to engage actively in diplomacy, travelling to Holland, France, Spain, and finally England, trying to arrange a new truce.

Rubens meanwhile did not abandon his primary vocation. During these years as a diplomat he still masterminded vast decorative projects, many of which had obvious political implications, such as the life cycle of Marie de Médicis for the Luxembourg Palace in Paris. These twenty-one paintings, some as large as twelve by twenty feet, were commissioned in 1621 and finished in 1625, in time for the reception given by Cardinal Richelieu for the marriage of Henrietta, daughter of Marie de Médicis, and Charles I of England (Slide 7). Marie chose Rubens for this herculean task because of his great fame and reputation for rapidity, though perhaps equally important was the fact there were no other painters in Europe capable of such an undertaking. The appointment was no doubt also politically motivated: Marie was on good terms with Isabella, and since the series glorifies the French queen it may even be construed as a subtle attack on her independent chief minister Richelieu and his pro-Dutch policies. Indeed, Richelieu mistrusted Rubens and was responsible for cancelling Rubens' commission to do one more series, which was to pay tribute to Henry IV, for another wing of the Luxembourg; only some sketches for this cycle remain (Slide 8) and two large unfinished pictures in the Uffizi.

The Marie de Médicis series is one of the largest programmatic decorations in the world, well justifying Delacroix's pronouncement that Rubens was the Homer of painting. It was the first of its kind by a northern painter since this field up to then had been the province of the Italians; the closest parallel in France at the time was the *Galerie François Premier* in the palace of Fontainebleau, dating from the mid-sixteenth century, which was the work of the Italian Mannerists Rosso Fiorentino and Primaticcio. Although the Médicis series was done in collaboration with pupils, we know that Rubens himself finished some of the canvases *in situ* and that he had the final hand in all of them. Rubens used allegory and fable to dress up the rather uninspiring program he was given, transforming the prosaic events in Marie's life into a series of glorious tableaux that would have done honor to the most exalted of monarchs. The series definitely confirmed Rubens' greatness to all, and his fame quickly spread throughout the whole of Europe. The influence of this cycle on succeeding generations was enormous. In seventeenth-century France, for example, Rubens was to become the rallying cry of those painters, such as Rigaud and Largillière, who fought the Academy's insistence on the supremacy of form over color; they were called "rubénistes" and their opponents, the partisans of form and line, "poussinistes," after Nicolas Poussin.

Lest the reader be lulled into thinking that the enormous Marie de Médicis series took up all the time and energy of Rubens, he should know that the master continued to distribute his genius with the same prodigality as ever. Canvas after canvas poured out of his fecund imagination. This is the time, for example, of *The Adoration of the Magi* (Slide 6), the tapestry designs commissioned in 1622 by Louis XIII of France illustrating the history of Constantine (Figure 14), and the cartoons for the tapestry series of *The Triumph of the Eucharist* ordered by Isabella.

However, in the mid 1620s we can speak for the first time of a slackening in Rubens' artistic production. These years brought him even more intense and personal sorrow than the continued destruction of Flanders. In 1623 he lost his daughter, Clara Serena, and three years later his wife and beloved companion. Rubens now actively sought diplomatic appointments to take his mind off his grief.

In 1626 he wrote: "I believe that a journey would be the best means of distracting my mind from many things which now of necessity renew my sorrow. . . ." He sold the bulk of his collection, including the Carleton antiquities, to the Duke of Buckingham, and after a brief and fruitless mission in Holland he left as an envoy to Spain in 1628. He soon enjoyed the full confidence and hospitality of Philip IV, who came every day to see him paint. His very fruitful nine-month stay at the Spanish court marked a turning point in his career. Once again Rubens seems to have been deeply affected by the art of Titian, and he made numerous copies after the superb paintings by this master in the King's collection; the highly pictorial, lyrical, and sunny qualities of Rubens' late works

Figure 14.

The Triumphal Entry of Constantine into Rome
tapestry, 191¾" x 214¼"
designed by Rubens, woven 1623-1625
Philadelphia Museum of Art

owe much to the great Venetian. During this visit Rubens also met Velásquez, court painter to Philip IV. Rubens' portraits of the king and queen, as well as the rest of the royal family, show a marked contrast with the more austere and reserved, the more monochromatic and silvery portraits of this immortal Spanish painter; they are more flamboyant and colorful but less subtle and penetrating.

It was not until his voyage to England in 1629, however, as the special envoy of Philip IV, that Rubens' diplomatic success was complete. In December of the following year a peace treaty was finally signed between Spain and England, and Rubens was knighted by James I for his efforts in the negotiations. The English king also commissioned him to decorate the Banqueting Hall at Whitehall (the old Westminster Palace), a vast undertaking that was only to be completed in 1634. Like the Marie de Médicis cycle it paid tribute to a reigning monarch and thus also called for complex and delicate iconography, wrought with political undertones. The ceiling, which was recently cleaned, is a glorious *tour de force,* sparkling in color; it is probably in great part by Rubens himself because its quality is very high and because it shows a number of variances from the sketches, which are amongst the artist's most spontaneous and masterful.

His return from England in 1630 spelled a new life for Rubens. After a final and bitterly disappointing failure in 1631 to resolve the conflict between Flanders and Holland which continued despite the peace between England and Spain, the artist at last implored Isabella to free him from his diplomatic duties: "I seized," he wrote, "the opportunity of a short secret journey to throw myself at the feet of Her Highness and pray her, as the only recompense for so many labors, to set me free of new undertakings. . . ." The year before, in 1630, the 53-year-old artist had married the sixteen-year-old radiant and blonde Helena Fourment, who was to become his favorite model. He justified this union to his friend Pereisc: "When I found I was not yet fitted for a life of celibacy, I resolved to get married again; and as we give the first prize to continence, we may enjoy lawful pleasure, for which we give thanks." Rubens bought a chateau in the country at Steen, where he spent the summers. His felicity was marred only by his increasingly painful attacks of "gout," probably a form of the rheumatism from which he had already suffered in the twenties, and by his genuine sorrow at the state of his "beloved Flanders" now in the throes of the worst destructive forces of the Thirty Years War.

Rubens' glorious paintings during these difficult years are a hymn to God's creation and the regeneration of life, a great, radiant cry of joyful optimism in the midst of suffering and gloom. His last works do not appear to be dictated so much by the milieu and by public demands and reflect very strongly, and most intimately, Rubens' own personal view of the world. He abandons himself more than ever to the pleasures of the physical world and with a disconcertingly healthy and frank attitude sharpens all his senses to capture it in all its varying facets. The majority of the late works are mythologies and fables of an unrestrainedly joyful mood, bursting with light and unabashed sensuality.

These lyrical outbursts, though, are occasionally punctuated by more dramatic, some-

Figure 15.
The Way to Calvary
(1636-1637)
oil on canvas
224″ x 139¾″
Musées Royaux des Beaux-Arts
Brussels

times violent subjects—undoubtedly caused by the artist's continued pained reaction to the pillage and carnage in Flanders. Still, it is Rubens' irreducible, immutable optimism that triumphs: the dead Christ on the Cross is not an image of gloom; He has the majestic air of one who will triumph in his very death. Among the greatest of the late religious compositions is the gigantic *Way to Calvary* in Brussels (Figure 15). One of the most glorious expressions of the Baroque, it has lost none of the virile strength and vigor of the earlier works. All is movement, which sweeps us through the spiralling, surging rhythm, now no longer so sculptural, but expressed by light and color. The strong local tones still present in *The Adoration of the Magi* of 1624 (Slide 6) are now broken up in a myriad of broad, excited brushstrokes and fused in a strong, even light. The diagonal composition climbs toward Golgotha where Christ, bent under the weight of the Cross, is going to a shameful death; yet the very sweep of its movement, along with the glory of color, takes us past the momentary anguish of Christ to foretell his final victory.

If Rubens' love of life can be seen in even the most somber of subjects, how much more clearly is it expressed in the numerous paintings of his deliciously alluring young wife Helena. Helena in her radiant nudity parades unashamedly in utterly ravishing pictures in which the sensuality of the subject is matched by that of the *matière*—by the sheer delight Rubens obviously took in the application of the paint itself in broad, fluid strokes. Helena is perhaps all three graces (Slide 15), she is resplendent as *Bathsheba* in Dresden, audacious in *La Petite Pelisse* (Slide 18), and in spirit everywhere in the *Offering to Venus,* a veritable testimonial to Titian, whose *putti* Rubens has sprinkled lovingly over the entire surface of the canvas.

The portraits and landscapes of these last years also exude the same warmth and richness. His lush, generous landscapes (Slide 12) reflect his deep love for the Flemish soil and the rolling, fertile valleys of Elewijt, where he spent a good deal of time at his chateau in Steen; in 1635 he wrote: "I now lead a life full of serenity in the company of my wife and my children, and my sole desire is to continue living in peace." This serenity is reflected in his many portraits of his family (Slide 17). These have a new intimacy, warmth, and psychological insight as yet undeveloped in the earlier, more formal portraits in which Rubens had sought to flatter his models and to characterize them not so much as individuals but according to their profession or rank in society; outward appearance, pose, costume, and surroundings were of prime importance (Slide 10). These earlier portraits, for the most part painted at various courts, are often the least inspired of his efforts. Indeed, as early as 1603 Rubens had begged the Duke of Mantua not to commission him to paint portraits, perhaps because he did not enjoy painting them as much as the multi-figured compositions which provided the most rewarding outlet for his powerful imagination.

Though Rubens now suffered cruelly from the "gout," he managed to fulfill with more brilliance than ever the deluge of commissions that still rained upon him. In 1634-35 he had been asked to supervise and design the decorations for the triumphal entry into Antwerp of the Cardinal Infante Ferdinand, the brother of Philip IV, and the new governor of

Figure 16.
Sketch for a Triumphal Chariot
(1638)
oil on wood, 40½″ x 28″
Musée Royal des Beaux-Arts
Antwerp

the Spanish Netherlands. It was a herculean task demanding extraordinary organizational talent, and the total success of the enterprise is again proof of Rubens' universal genius and enormous power of invention. In only a few days time he poured out designs for triumphal arches, grandstands, statues, paintings, and banners, all to be erected in the streets of Antwerp. Some of the sketches are preserved and they are of truly epic grandeur (Figure 16); even the architecture of twisted columns and heavy pediments pulsates with life.

Before his death Rubens embarked on one of his most monumental undertakings, that of providing designs for more than 100 paintings, many illustrating scenes from Ovid, for the decoration of Philip IV's hunting lodge, and to which Velásquez also contributed (Slide 16). Only a few of the paintings were finished by Rubens himself, but the preliminary sketches are perhaps the most vivid and fresh we have from his hand. This hand, so nimble and alive, and to which we owe some of the most heavenly pictures in the world, could be stilled only by death. Rubens died on the 30th of May, 1640.

In his incredibly full life he seems to have drained his nation's artistic genius; his olympian breath was to stifle the succeeding generations. Too difficult to equal, he had no direct heirs. But outside Flanders, and in different ages, his genius was to be rekindled in Watteau, Delacroix, and finally Renoir, whose rich, sun-drenched palette and opulent nudes take up again, in a new form, the positive, joyful message of Rubens.

COMMENTARY ON THE SLIDES

COMMENTARY ON THE SLIDES

1: THE DESCENT FROM THE CROSS (1612), oil on wood
165¾″ x 122½″, Antwerp Cathedral

The Descent from the Cross is the center of a triptych painted for the Cathedral of Notre Dame in Antwerp. The *Descent* was completed in 1612 and the wings, probably with the help of assistants, in 1614. It is characteristic of Rubens' early classicizing manner and borrows extensively from Italian Mannerist prototypes. But what is important is that all the foreign elements are completely assimilated and reshaped into pure Rubens. Although the figures, a bit bloated and turgid as in all of Rubens' early works, are strongly and individually modeled, it is the unity of conception, the dynamic diagonal sweep of the composition, its single binding rhythm, which are most striking and modern. The only real concession to late Mannerist vision is the deliberate arrangement of the figures in a single plane and the high polish and finish of the surface. The important role played here by Mary Magdalen, who holds the feet of Christ, is symptomatic of the Counter-Reformation, which stirred interest in this figure who traditionally represented the repentant sinner. Especially touching is the direct, even physical, confrontation of the Magdalen with her Redeemer, an element that causes the onlooker to identify further with the Magdalen and become closely involved with the action.

2: THE RAPE OF THE DAUGHTERS OF LEUCIPPUS (1615-1617)
oil on canvas, 87½″ x 82¼″, Alte Pinakothek, Munich

In this exceptionally beautiful and animated composition Rubens makes a masterly and dramatic use of oppositions. They are evident here in every aspect of the painting, from the manner in which the mythological story is depicted to the handling of the paint. The painting represents the abduction of the daughters of Leucippus at their wedding ceremony by the illustrious twin sons of Zeus, Castor and Pollux. The girls, Phoebe and Milaira, appear to put up relatively little resistance, and their attempt to invoke the gods is really half-hearted. Set before a gently rolling Flemish landscape, one might think it a blown-up detail from the *Flemish Kermesse* (Slide 13) and not a mythological subject at all, except for the nudity of the girls and the battle dress of the twins. The calm setting, along with the cupid attending the reins of one of the horses, points to the peaceful outcome of the story, for this stormy episode will resolve itself in the marriage of the daughters to the twins. One writer has remarked rather poetically that the victors indeed appear to have been vanquished already.

In both the composition and the painting technique, the most expressive element is the use of counterpoint. The light, enamel-like colors of the women's skin tones, for example, are set off by the swarthy complexions of Castor and Pollux, their contrasts of coloring again repeated in the pelts of the horses. Rubens' delight in playing off every texture is amply illustrated by the differentiations of the armor, drapery, flesh, and animal hides. Similar contrasts are found within the composition; strongly accented diagonals are balanced by countermovements which maintain a stable sense of organization despite the strong centrifugal movement. This beautiful and spirited composition is one of Rubens' most lucid, and in few other pictures is the cerebral ordering so clearly felt underneath the outward appearance of sound and fury.

3:   LION AND WOLF HUNT (1617-1618), oil on canvas
98″ x 147⅔″, Alte Pinakothek, Munich

This impressive, explosive picture was painted for Maximilian, Duke of Bavaria, perhaps with the help of Van Dyck. Its subject was one that provided Rubens with an ideal outlet for his unbridled energy and dynamism. The ferocious clash of men and animals is brought out with great realism, and the impact is made most effective by the placement of the action at our eye level, as if we were in the hunt itself. Tumultuous yet not disorderly, the sense of confusion and wildness is tempered by the brilliantly thought-out composition. The dominant movement is the dramatic diagonal of the rider falling off his horse; but in order that our eyes are not forced beyond the picture frame, the hunter clad in red on the left and the fallen hunter on the right help balance this diagonal and square off the composition. All parts project outward, radiating toward the outside; the pell mell array of horses, men, and wild beasts is so violently torn from the center of the composition toward the sides that the docile rectangle of the canvas seems scarcely able to contain it.

Delacroix, who admired Rubens enormously, felt excessive confusion and disorder in this picture, and his own lion hunts, patterned on Rubens', are indeed tamer. But we have seen that the frantic action here is not total chaos; it is calculated by a strong intellect capable of balancing an impetuous temperament.

4: MADONNA AND CHILD IN A GARLAND OF FLOWERS (1616-1618)
oil on wood, 73" x 82⅔", Alte Pinakothek, Munich

This delicious picture was painted with the collaboration of Jan "Velvet" Brueghel, who is responsible for the sumptuous garland of flowers. Rubens painted a number of small devotional pictures in which he shows that he is capable of expressing tender sentiment and emotion. The Virgin, slightly withdrawn, averts our gaze and looks pensively down in a wonderful gesture of humility. She presents to us the chubby pink and dimpled Christ Child, who stands on her knee very naturally and looks at us with disarming eagerness and innocence. The Child is a favored type of Rubens and is based on the physiognomy of his own son Nicolas, born in 1618, whom he painted many times.

Rubens' wealth of invention is evident in the lively clusters of cherubs—who probably stand for the Holy Innocents—all in different and justly observed attitudes hovering playfully about the group of the Virgin and Child and holding up the garland.

5: LE COUP DE LANCE (1620), oil on wood, 169" x 122½"
Musée Royal des Beaux-Arts, Antwerp

The *Coup de Lance,* representing the dramatic moment when Longinus pierces the side of Christ, is perhaps Rubens' most famous religious picture. Commissioned by Burgomaster Nicolas Rockox in 1620 for the main altar of the Church of the Recollects in Antwerp, it brilliantly fulfilled the aims of the Counter-Reformation in the north—to inspire the spectator to greater religious fervor by involving him directly in the action.

Rubens has achieved this with rare and brutal realism. Note the horrible detail of the lifted flesh and gushing blood made by the lance's thrust into the side of Christ, and the unrepentant thief who, in the unbearable torment of having his bones broken by a soldier, has wrenched one foot free from the nails. His contortions contrast markedly with the beautiful but deathly still body of Christ, inundated by a shaft of light that also pours down onto the tear-drenched face of the imploring Magdalen. The Virgin here is standing at the foot of the Cross, not swooning as she was often shown in earlier representations of the Crucifixion; the Church now insisted on accurate reading of the scriptures, and the words in John 19:25 are: "Now there STOOD by the Cross of Jesus, his mother. . . ." The brilliant colors ranging from blood red to the golden yellow of the Magdalen's hair, the dashing execution, and the surging composition moving obliquely in space from left to right with great eloquence completely dominate the macabre anecdotal details and help make this somber and pathetic picture, a grand epic, a great hymn to the glory of God.

6: THE ADORATION OF THE MAGI (1624), oil on wood
176″ x 132″, Musée Royal des Beaux-Arts, Antwerp

The Adoration of the Magi, one of Rubens' greatest creations, was painted in 1624 for the high altar of St. Michael's Abbey in Antwerp. It is a great Baroque extravaganza, a veritable pageant, in which all the pomp of the Catholic Church in adoration before the Christ Child proclaims the glory of God with noise and ostentation in deliberate contrast to the Protestant austerity of Holland. The religious sentiment is not profound; here Rubens expresses his faith by stressing the outward drama, and he places the emphasis on the kings and their rich, exotic retinue. Saint Joseph is relegated to the penumbra on the right, almost out of the picture, while the center is dominated by the extraordinary figure of a giant Moorish king who faces frontward, only turning his eyes with awe and disbelief toward this tiny baby, King of the World. Towering on the left in a brilliant red coat, is the startling figure of a bearded magi who looks straight at the onlooker, thus involving him directly in the adoration; the third king, in a bright white mantel, kneels with great dignity and reverence before the Child, who is not sitting passively on his mother's knee, but eagerly reaches for his adorers in true Rubensian fashion.

All the elements in this densely crowded Baroque composition, so full of invention and mastery, are unified in one single élan. The procession of kings pours down onto the scene in a swirling motion which starts at the upper right with the enormous camels cut out against a bright sky, moves down to the left, rotates around the Moor, and crosses back toward the luminous area with the beautiful group of the Virgin and Child. All is large, opulent, and alive, a feast of warm colors, reds, golds, and greens, applied with brushstrokes of an incredible sureness and rapidity. It is a pictorial miracle, combining the solidity and density of forms characteristic of the early Rubens with the lightness of touch and painterly qualities of his late works.

7: THE LANDING OF MARIE DE MÉDICIS AT MARSEILLES (1622-1625)
oil on canvas, 156¼″ x 112″, Louvre, Paris

This is one of the paintings for the series *The Life of Marie de Médicis* painted for the Luxembourg in 1622-1625, in which history is associated with allegory and mythology as nymphs and goddesses join the queen in various episodes of her life. Here France, represented by a soldier with fleur-de-lys on his cloak, and the city of Marseilles, by a young woman, rush forth to greet the queen, while Fame hovers above sounding a trumpet. Below, Neptune and sea deities moor the boat and, in their spirited water dance and healthy blond glow, express the joyful greeting far better than the affected gestures of the allegorical figures or the courtiers. The bold upward surging of the naiads in the foreground leads with a powerful, sweeping movement to the figures above, the actual subject of the picture, and sets the rhythm for the whole painting.

The top of the composition may be the work of students but the naiads are surely by the master's own hand. They were probably painted in Paris since Rubens, in an undated letter, asks to have three models available in Paris in order to paint three life-size *sirènes*. We know these models had dark hair, but Rubens may later easily have changed two of them into blondes in the painting. Delacroix admired enormously these bold, luxurious nudes, which were thought a bit frank at the time; the Archduke Ferdinand is known to have regretted "the exceeding nudity of the three goddesses"—to which Rubens is said to have responded that they were nevertheless "good painting."

8: THE TRIUMPHAL ENTRY OF HENRY IV INTO PARIS (late 1620s)
oil on wood, 19½″ x 33″
Metropolitan Museum of Art, New York, Rogers Fund, 1942

This painting is the sketch for the much larger picture now in the Uffizi in Florence. It was destined to figure in a cycle celebrating the life of Henry IV (1553-1610) similar to the series on the life of Marie de Médicis that Rubens had just completed for the Luxembourg Palace. Due to political reasons it was never completed, and by 1630 Rubens had ceased working on it.

As in the Marie de Médicis series, Rubens combines fact and allegory in his depiction of Henry IV's triumphal entrance into Paris after his coronation at Chartres Cathedral in 1594. Of Huguenot origin, Henry had converted to Catholicism in order to be crowned king. He is shown here entering the Porte Neuve, riding alone in a golden quadriga pulled by white horses, the reins of which are held by the Roman goddess of war Bellona. Victory places a wreath on his head. Heeding Roman tradition, the king is acclaimed by the populace and followed by captives, presumably from the battle at Ivry where Henry defeated the Catholic armies of the Duc de Guises.

Intended to show his patron, Marie de Médicis, how the finished work would look, this sketch not only illustrates the genesis of the composition, but the genius of Rubens' painterly style. With marvelous spontaneity, Rubens drew directly with the brush over the initial preparation in bistre and gray, using colors dominated by pink and blue. The brush seems to glide over the warm background, letting the golden priming show through and drawing in its wake grand and clearly articulated swarms of figures. It is astonishing how rich an impression of pictorial brilliance Rubens can create with a few notes of color on a golden-brown base. With only a few strokes he can construct a figure, its gesture, movement, and weight completely expressed. Rubens doesn't bother with details; it is the relation of the parts to the whole and the general expression and movement that counts. A single impetuous movement unifies and gives coherence to the entire composition.

9: ALBERT AND NICOLAS RUBENS (c. 1625-1626), oil on wood
62¼″ x 36¼″, Liechtenstein Gallery, Vaduz

This sumptuous and elegant portrait of the artist's two sons, Albert (b. 1614) and Nicolas (b. 1618), was painted at the peak of Rubens' fame and success. Honored, rich, and firmly entrenched in the position of ambassador-at-large, he had just completed the enormous Marie de Médicis cycle, for which he received much acclaim. His fulfillment, as well as his fatherly love and pride, is amply expressed in this portrait. A masterpiece of pictorial splendor and psychological insight, the portrait involves a rare combination of pomp and theatricality with intimacy and truth. Charmingly pretentious on the one hand, with the children shown *en grande tenue,* it is still its candor and freshness which are most striking.

Nicolas holds a goldfinch at the end of a string, and Rubens sets off his bright, variegated costume and his roguish, playful face against the dark coat of Albert, who looks very much like his mother Isabella. He is depicted as a student, holding a book in his right hand, and also acts a bit the part of a *Grand Seigneur,* surely copying his father in affecting the stylish gesture of the glove in hand, while at the same time his arm rests protectively on his brother's shoulder. The clamorous but not discordant colors of Nicolas' costume give accent and brilliance to the picture, which is luminous in its harmonies of browns and blacks. The young and lithe silhouettes of the boys are rendered especially alive in contrast to the weighty, massive column, a standard device of state portraiture, and the shadowy background serves as a perfect foil for their light, expressive faces. The portrait is more mannered than later ones, such as *Helena Fourment and her Children* (Slide 17), but it is enormously sympathetic and imbued with life, as expressed in the flaring nostrils, the expressive mouths and the laughing eyes. The strong carnation of the flesh tones makes us understand how the Bolognese Baroque painter Guido Reni could say that Rubens "mixed blood with his colors."

10: PORTRAIT OF GASPARD GEVARTIUS (c. 1628), oil on wood
47″ x 38½″, Musée Royal des Beaux-Arts, Antwerp

Gaspard Gevartius was the communal secretary of Antwerp, and he shared with Rubens a fondness for philosophy and literature. Rubens portrayed him in the customary formula for depicting a humanist, who is usually shown reading or writing, surrounded by the appurtenances of his profession. Here Gevartius, who is about to put pen to paper, sits among his prized books, and on his desk is a bust of the Roman Emperor Marcus Aurelius, a symbolical allusion to the Stoical maxims and thinking favored by both Gevartius and Rubens.

In typical Baroque fashion, this portrait establishes a direct and clear confrontation between the portrayed and the spectator: the sitter turns toward the onlooker and focuses his attention on him. The personality of Gevartius is relayed to us, not through an inward and psychological study of his features, but through the setting and his gestures. Although the pose is rather formal, the painting is given a great deal of vitality through the strong, level gaze and sensitive hands of Gevartius. In his expressive face especially, the touches of red and brown contrast vividly with the shiny, rich, deep blacks of his clothing.

It was Gevartius who in 1630 publicly sang the praises of Helena Fourment's beauty and who in 1642 published an account of the entry of Ferdinand into Antwerp, another pageant which had been masterminded by **Rubens.**

11:   GARDEN OF LOVE (1632-1634), oil on canvas
78″ x 111½″, Prado, Madrid

The *Garden of Love* is in a sense the antithesis of the *Flemish Kermesse* (Slide 13), substituting an elegant society for the Flemish peasants. All that was primitive and direct in the *kermesse* is disposed here in more refined, aristocratic gestures, and Rubens has thoughtfully supplied urging *amors* for the ladies who are about to succumb to the advances of the gallant men. This admirable picture is the very summary of Rubens' optimism and love of life. It is probably also rather autobiographical; we can be permitted to recognize Rubens in the dashing figure on the left, Helena in the figure seated in the center resting her arm on another's knees, and her archetype in different guises in all the women. The architecture is similar to that of Rubens' own house in Antwerp, and symbols of matrimony—a yoke, turtle doves, etc. held by an *amor* on the left—punctuate this free love scene.

Called at the time, a *conversation à la mode,* this painting is in the tradition of the Venetion bucolic landscapes and the forerunner of Watteau's *fêtes galantes.* Rubens must have especially cherished this earthly paradise as there exist a number of variants, and it was made into his largest and most elaborate woodcut. The drawing for it is in the Metropolitan Museum of Art and the woodcut was executed by Jeghers. This opulent, yet highly civilized and distinguished monument to love is well worthy of a king's chamber; indeed it was bought by Philip IV of Spain at the posthumous Rubens' sale and was hung in his bedroom.

12:   LANDSCAPE WITH A RAINBOW (mid 1630s), oil on wood
37¼″ x 48½″, Alte Pinakothek, Munich

John Constable, the eighteenth-century English painter, once said of Rubens' landscapes: "Rubens delighted in phenomena." Indeed, for Rubens landscape was fascinating only when it offered him a chance to paint dramatic effects of light and capture the cosmic forces of nature. He loved to paint nature in a state of flux, often at sunset or, as here, after the rain when the sun pierces through the clouds to innundate with light and life the rolling hills of Flanders. Just as Rubens' feminine type had generous forms, so he stressed in his landscapes the fecundity of the earth; there are no winter scenes, only nature at its richest moments when the trees are swollen with sap and the earth yields its fruits to man.

Though Rubens painted some landscapes early in his career, the majority date from his last years, when he was spending more time in the country. This landscape is painted in the broad, loose manner of his mature style, and the topography is reminiscent of that near his country house at Steen. Massive forms or architecture seldom appear in his landscapes, where all is organic and in motion. The high point of view and vast expanses of these works hark back to the tradition of Peter Brueghel.

13: FLEMISH KERMESSE (1635-1638), oil on wood
58⅔″ x 102¾″, Louvre, Paris

This remarkable peasant scene underscores the strong kinship that exists between Rubens and Peter Brueghel (c. 1529-1569), another intensely Flemish artist. Since Brueghel's time, the village feast had become a favorite subject of Flemish artists, the most notable of whom were David Teniers and Adrian Brouwer. Rubens' temperament and position led him to more exalted subjects, yet he did paint two peasant scenes, this one and another in the Prado.

Rubens knew Breughel's art well. He owned at least twelve of the master's works, as well as some by Teniers and Brouwer. The difference between the latters' passion for detail and anecdotal description and Rubens' more cosmic vision is indeed striking. Peasants interested Rubens only insofar as they displayed a primordial energy untempered by social and formal restraints. While Brueghel tended to categorize the peasants into types, Rubens grasped their immediate and individual reality. The direct opposite of the more refined and civilized *Garden of Love* (Slide 11), this painting treats the Flemish sense of well-being at a primitive, unrestrained level where the participants of the *kermesse* freely indulge their many appetites.

It is perhaps one of Rubens' most complex compositions. Spellbinding rhythms swirl like eddies back and forth across the canvas. René Huygue, former curator at the Louvre, has described it beautifully: "Everything jostles everything else and winds in and out in a farandole, like a chain that makes a thousand turns in order to fill up every corner of the canvas." Every figure is caught up in this movement of life. Art intervened here, of course, and nothing, not even the poses and expressions, are fortuitous. Rubens submitted his figures to his own secret law that expresses, more strongly perhaps than any other, the fundamental rhythms of life.

14: THE HORRORS OF WAR (1637-1638), oil on canvas
81" x 136", Palazzo Pitti, Florence

The complex allegorical meaning of this painting is explained by Rubens himself in a letter of 1638 to the painter Justus Sustermans, unusual for its rare, detailed description of one of his own works: "The principal figure is Mars who . . . rushes forth with shield and bloodstained sword, threatening the people with great disaster. He pays little heed to Venus, his mistress, who, accompanied by her Amors and Cupids, strives with caresses and embraces to hold him. From the other side, Mars is dragged forward by the fury Aleko, with a torch in her hand. Nearby are monsters personifying Pestilence and Famine . . ." Further described are Harmony, Fecundity, Architecture, Arts and Letters, and Concord, all threatened or destroyed by war, and "that grief-stricken woman clothed in black, with torn veil, robbed of all her jewels and other ornaments, is the unfortunate Europe who, for so many years now, has suffered plunder, outrage, and misery. . . ."

The painting was executed some time before 1638 and expresses with agonizing realism and power Rubens' own grief at the sight of his "beloved Flanders" in the midst of the worst excesses of the Thirty Years War. Here, as in *The Triumphal Entry Of Henry IV into Paris* (Slide 8), the composition moves with great force laterally—not in a swirling movement as in *The Rape of the Daughters of Leucippus* (Slide 2), or radiating explosively as in the *Lion and Wolf Hunt* (Slide 3)—but in a side thrust across the canvas. The contrast of the cold, hard armor of Mars and the soft, warm flesh of Venus, the blood-red cloak, the purplish-blue smoke rising on the right, and the distant orange glow of fire, all contribute forcefully to create a mood of true drama, horror, and violence. The painting is brushed with unusual vigor and swiftness, so much so that it has been criticized for faulty drawing and weak modeling; but its strong color harmonies, inexorable movement, and pictorial brilliance make it certainly one of the most vivid and compelling statements of the horrors of war.

15: THE THREE GRACES (c. 1639), oil on wood
87" x 71¼", Prado, Madrid

An homage to his own conception of female beauty, this painting of the three graces epitomizes the opulent, generous, and sensual characteristics Rubens sought in his female nudes, as well as in his painting technique. Although representing the three "protectors of philosophers," Rubens has used the subject as a pretext to set off the soft, opalescent flesh tones of the luxurious nudes against a dark landscape background. Rubens found his ideal feminine form in his two wives, Isabella and Helena. Here Helena posed for the grace on the left, although all three share her charms. It is interesting to note that all three graces are posed in a manner very similar to that of Helena in *La Petite Pelisse* (Slide 18).

Rubens has created here a veritable *tour de force.* He seems to be feasting on the multivariety of iridescent reflections on the skin tones, made ever so much more vibrant by their silhouette against the sky and landscape (which may be the work of an assistant). The light is soft and general in order to keep shadows to a minimum so that all attention is drawn to the milky whites and tender pinks. And, as if it were not noticeable, Rubens further emphasizes the amplitude of the figures, which seem about to dance, by such virtuoso techniques as the pressure of the thumb of the central nude into the arm of another. It was surely these rich effects that pleased Philip IV, who acquired the painting at the posthumous Rubens' sale.

16: VENUS AND ADONIS (late 1630s), oil on canvas, 77½" x 94½"
Metropolitan Museum of Art, New York, Gift of Harry Payne Bingham, 1937

Taken from Ovid's *Metamorphoses,* this picture may well have been intended for Philip IV's hunting lodge, since it shows Venus vainly trying to dissuade the handsome shepherd Adonis, of whom she is enamored, from leaving for a hunt of wild beasts which she knows will be fatal. Even the magic weapons of her cohort Cupid have proved useless, and he has tossed them to the ground. In a desperate, touching gesture he clutches tightly the sinewy thigh of Adonis.

Another late work, this luxuriant picture shows again the subtle role that Titian plays in the creative process of Rubens. Rubens had copied a painting of the same subject by Titian (now in the Prado) in 1628, but here he has transformed it by his painting technique and bright, limpid colors into something strictly his own. The pearly white body of the goddess is set off sharply against the swarthy coloring of the shepherd, and both, marvelously fluid in movement, sway before a lush, light-flecked landscape which, like the figures, is surely by the master's hand. The highlights on the flesh show how well Rubens understood reflected light. A marvelous blend of form and color has been achieved by subtle gradations of color and light, which also cause the masterly transitions from flesh to cloth to landscape. The figures and the sentiment are especially noble, and made this grand picture a most princely gift indeed; it was, in fact, given by Joseph I, Emperor of Germany, to John, Duke of Marlborough.

17: HELENA FOURMENT AND HER CHILDREN (1636-1637)
oil on wood, 44½" x 32¼", Louvre, Paris

This is one of the most appealing of Rubens' portraits; it conveys a unique mood of tenderness and joy, as well as a serenity rare for the artist, which no doubt reflects the happiness of his last years spent in relative peace with his family and away from the turmoil of diplomatic activity. It was probably painted in 1636-1637, judging from the ages of the children: Claire-Jeanne, standing, would be four and François, on his mother's lap, three. To the right a baby's hand holding on to the chair is sketched in, probably that of one-year-old Isabelle-Claire.

Rubens may have intended to enlarge the picture to accommodate more, but in its unfinished state it has all the freshness of a sketch. It is very light in tone, a ravishing harmony in pearly grays and blacks set off against the warm red of the chair and accented by the touches of blue in the background. It is brushed with prodigious assurance and effortless ease; in its shimmering light and delicacy of touch it has all the marks of an improvisation. Much of the portrait's force and poetry derives from the avoidance of the anecdotal; the attitudes of the children are wonderfully natural and Helena, whose expression is strangely pensive, does not focus on any one thing. This is a maternity scene with universal appeal, not a specific instance in the relationship between mother and children. The painting has marvelous unity of tone and feeling and the overall golden-brown tonality is perfectly suited to its mood. Renoir copied this portrait, and no wonder, as its warmth and intimacy do anticipate him.

18: LA PETITE PELISSE, also known as THE FUR CLOAK (c. 1638)
oil on wood, 69¼" x 32⅔", Kunsthistorisches Museum, Vienna

Like the portrait of Helena Fourment and her children (Slide 17), this painting is one of Rubens' most intimate creations. More than just a portrait, it is perhaps the most perfect and complete expression of the love he held for his second wife, to whom he left this painting in his will.

All is life and motion, which he achieved with the half-lifted foot, the half-turned body, the contraposto of the folded arms, and the swinging arc of the fur mantle. Through subtle and artful ways Rubens has infused movement into the warmth and intimacy of the portrait. Helena may not necessarily have been painted as she stepped out of her bath, as is most often written, but instead may have simply draped herself with a cloak as she posed. In any case, there is no hint of academic formality, essentially because Rubens did not paint Helena as an ideal nude in the classical sense. On the contrary, he painted the naturalness of the woman he loved, the woman who brought joy to his last years, and who bore him five children. She is shown in a touchingly and unexpectedly modest pose, seeming vulnerable in her near nakedness.

The idea of this picture was probably derived from Titian's *Girl in a Fur Cloak* which Rubens must have seen in London in 1630 when it was in the collection of Charles I. But, transformed under Rubens' brush and temperament, *La Petite Pelisse* can be considered no more than a recollection of Titian's portrait.

19: SELF-PORTRAIT (1638-1640), oil on canvas
43″ x 33½″, Kunsthistorisches Museum, Vienna

In April 1640, Rubens wrote: "If I were not detained by my age and the gout which cripples me. . . ." These terrible words, penned by one of the most energetic and creative of men, are clearly shown in this superb and moving portrait; the melancholy look in the eyes is inescapable, although Rubens feigns a strong, sustained gaze. With a touch of vanity, Rubens has kept a glove on his gout-crippled hand, yet even the bare left hand does not hold the pommel of the sword but rests wearily on it. In this last self-portrait, the drawn face and tired eyes contrast sharply with the cocked hat and ample, theatrical cloak, the very same dashing accoutrements Rubens included in earlier self-portraits.

Unlike Rembrandt, who was much more introspective, Rubens painted few self-portraits. This one takes its place along with *La Petite Pelisse* as a most intimate portrayal, though perhaps the preparatory drawing in the Louvre, in which the artist does not wear a sword, is even more penetrating. In the painted version, it is Rubens as we know him from the writer-engraver Roger de Piles' description: "He was very large, his bearing majestic, of regular features, ruddy-cheeked, dark-haired, eyes brilliant but with a tempered fire; his smiling appearance gentle and straightforward."

20: STUDIES OF A NEGRO (c. 1620)
oil on wood, transferred to canvas, 20″ x 26″
Musées Royaux des Beaux-Arts, Brussels

Compositional studies by Rubens, such as this admirable essay into the physiognomy of a Negro, are few since Rubens usually composed directly from the model or from the images of his prodigious memory. This dynamically composed sketch, which in its artful figural placement announces the red chalk studies of Watteau, also carefully composed on the page, shows at once the enormous skill of the painter, as well as his keen penetration of human nature. Pictorially, these four heads are molded in swift, broad strokes which create in a direct and spontaneous way their movement and volume. The light gray-blues, ochres, and browns are a pure delight. However, Rubens did more than make a virtuoso study of the Negro's "novel" physiognomy. He explored his mentality and caught with extraordinary sharpness his seriousness and joviality, his anguish, and the look of astonishment that an African must have borne on first entering the modern, bustling city of Antwerp. The model in question must have posed for many artists toward 1620 since he can be recognized in works by Jordaens and notably by Van Dyck, to whom this study has been often attributed, mostly because of its delicate color scheme; however, the sureness and brio with which it is painted point unmistakably to Rubens.